Contents

Pictures of an overcrowded planet	2
The population clock is ticking	4
Population hotspots	6
Not enough food	8
Not enough water	12
Overcrowded cities	14
An overcrowded planet	16
The Earth is being spoiled	20
What can be done?	26
Glossary	30
Further information	31
Index	32

POP CLOCK: WHO ARE WE?

We are an organisation who have produced this book to try to persuade you that the world's population is growing too fast! We hope that when you've read the book and looked at the websites at the back you'll think about what you can do to help!

Pictures of an overcrowded planet

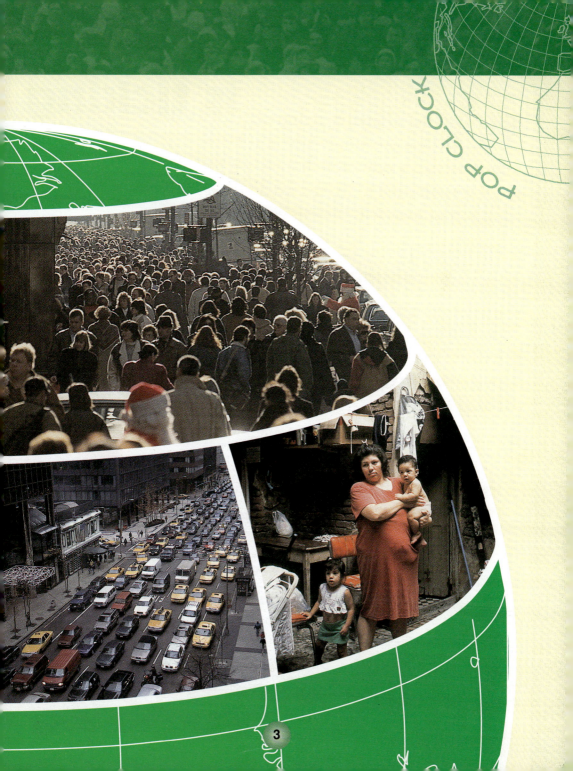

The population clock is ticking

The number of people living on the Earth is growing every day. Every minute of every day more babies are born. But if we continue to live as we do now, what sort of lives will they have? Already:

- millions of people are poor and die of hunger.

- the land, air and water are polluted. Animals become **extinct** every year because people are destroying the places where they live.

- the way people live is changing the planet's weather, causing floods and **droughts**.

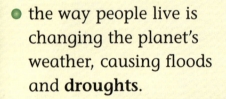

By 1999, there were six billion human beings on Earth.

6,000,000,000

By the year 2050, there could be eleven billion people. If the population goes on growing at this rate, in 900 years' time, we would need a building 2,000 floors high covering the whole planet to house everyone.

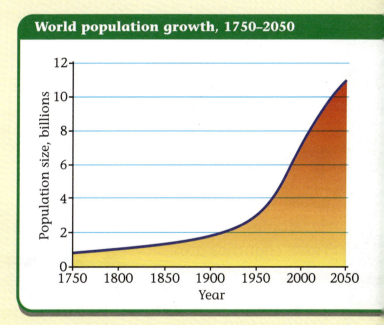

World population growth, 1750–2050

We are already facing many problems because there are too many people on the Earth. We must do something to help the people of the world who are suffering now. We must do something to protect our future on Earth, because the **population clock** is ticking like a time bomb.

Population hotspots

The world's population is growing at the fastest rate in the **developing countries**. These countries are known as 'population hotspots'. It is in these countries that the people are suffering the most today.

Ten countries or areas with the highest population density in 1999

Country or area	Population per square kilometre
1 Macau	25,942
2 Hong Kong	6,508
3 Singapore	5,699
4 Gaza Strip	2,850
5 Malta	1,222
6 Maldives	934
7 Bahrain	894
8 Bangladesh	882
9 Barbados	626
10 Mauritius	564

There are 4.8 billion people living in developing countries.

- Nearly two thirds of these people do not have proper toilets and washing rooms.
- Almost one third does not have clean water.
- About one quarter does not have proper housing.

Number of people people per square kilometre across the world

One square kilometre

Average

Australia

Asia

If the whole population was spread evenly across all the countries of the world, there would be about forty people living on each square kilometre. But, in Australia, there are just two people on each square kilometre, while in Asia there are seventy.

Not enough food

If the population goes on growing so quickly, we will not have enough food to go round. Already, millions of people in the world go hungry. But every year there are millions more mouths to feed.

Grains like wheat, rice and maize are a **staple food** for people in many countries. So to feed the population, we should produce more grain. Yet, the amount of grain we produce per person is falling.

Farmland has been over-used and *pesticides* do not work as well on insects which damage the crops.

Farmland has also been built on, because people need houses, factories, shopping centres and motorways.

We catch so many fish that soon the seas will be empty. Nearly three quarters of the most important fishing grounds in the world are being too heavily fished. Several types of fish, like tuna and cod, used to be common: now their numbers are falling. If too many fish are caught all at once, there are not enough left to breed, so the fish population goes down.

This is what is happening when the world population is six billion. If we don't make a change, what will happen to the farmland and the fish when the population is ten billion or more?

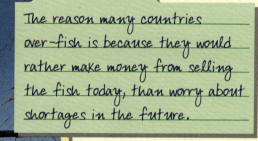

The reason many countries over-fish is because they would rather make money from selling the fish today, than worry about shortages in the future.

Some people protest about over-fishing.

Not enough water

All living things need water to live. As the human population grows, there won't be enough water to go around. We are using more and more water all the time: for farming, for industry, and in our homes. But the world has only a limited supply of water. What will happen when it runs out?

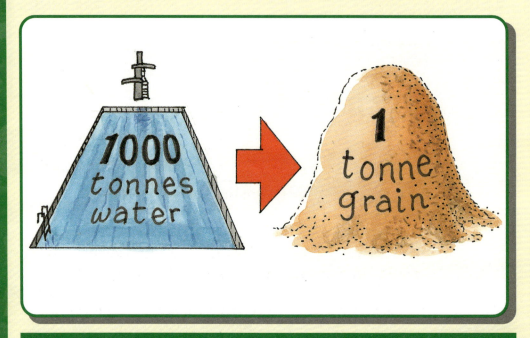

It takes 1,000 tons of water to produce just one ton of grain. A water shortage would also mean a food shortage.

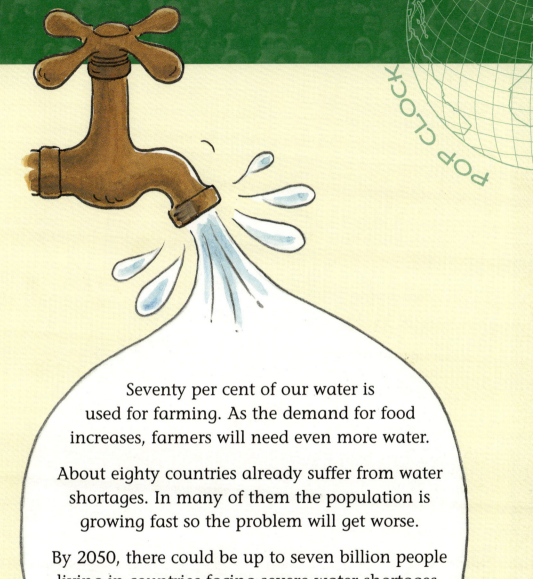

Seventy per cent of our water is used for farming. As the demand for food increases, farmers will need even more water.

About eighty countries already suffer from water shortages. In many of them the population is growing fast so the problem will get worse.

By 2050, there could be up to seven billion people living in countries facing severe water shortages.

Britain uses nine times more water per person per year than countries where water is scarce.

Overcrowded cities

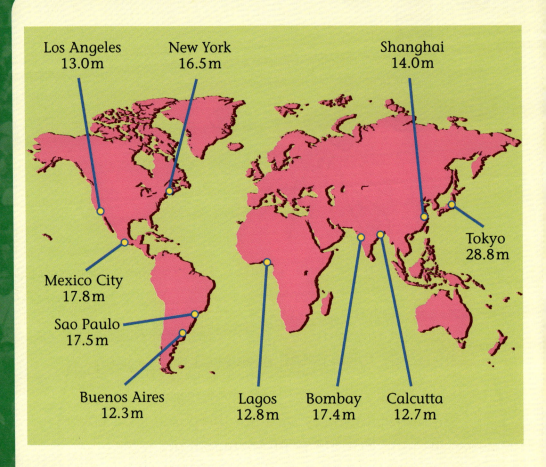

People move to cities because there are jobs there. As the population of a country increases, more and more people move to live in cities. But as cities get bigger and bigger, they become less and less pleasant to live in. There are not enough houses for the people and there is not enough clean water. When people live close together, diseases spread more easily. Cities are often full of pollution, poverty and homelessness.

Mexico City is a **megacity**. It is the biggest megacity in the developing world. It has a population of 17.8 million.
The air is so polluted that on some days schools and factories have to close and cars drive with their headlights on to see through the **smog**.

As the world's population increases, there could be more and more megacities in the world, and they could have the same problems.

Smog in Mexico City

An overcrowded planet

We all need space around us. As the population goes on growing, and more parts of the world become overcrowded, the problems of unemployment, crime and violence will also increase.

Today there are about one hundred and fifty million people in the world who have no job. If the population goes on growing, there will be even more people out of work. In Mexico alone, a million more jobs are needed each year for the growing population.

Without a job people do not have enough money.

A destroyed home in Rwanda.

Overcrowding can even lead to war between peoples sharing a country. In Rwanda, one of the most crowded countries in Africa, wars have killed a million people and destroyed forests and farmland. One of the reasons behind the wars is overcrowding. The different groups of native peoples fight each other because there is not enough food to eat, water for drinking and growing crops, or land to farm.

Around the world there are now about thirty wars and many smaller conflicts. In many cases they are caused by the fact that there are too many people in too small a space. So the people are fighting for limited **resources**.

Wars put people's lives in danger. Not just the soldiers, but the families whose homes are destroyed too.

The Earth is being spoiled

We are spoiling our planet because there are too many of us. More people use more food, water and fuel, and create more waste and pollution. They need more houses, hospitals, roads, schools, parks and playgrounds. They need more factories, offices and shopping centres.

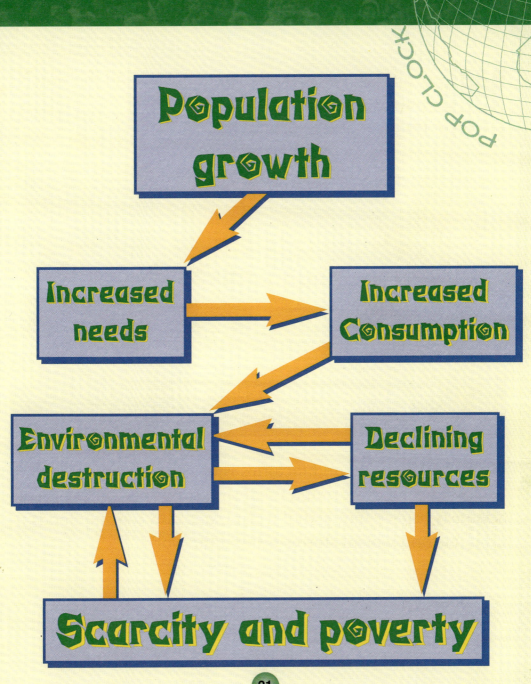

We are already polluting the land, the air and the water. Chemicals are destroying the **ozone layer** that protects the Earth from the Sun's harmful rays.

The build up of gases in the earth's atmosphere means more of the sun's energy is trapped. This energy heats up the earth more and causes global warming.

Burning fuel in cars and factories is causing **global warming**. Global warming is causing the sea levels to rise. Scientists believe that global warming is also causing floods, droughts and violent storms around the world.

Many of the world's biggest cities, are at risk from flooding. Floods can destroy huge areas of housing and farmland.

In other places, drought causes crops to die and people to starve.

In the last century, people destroyed a third of the world's forests. Forests are cut down to provide timber. Sometimes they are cut down to make space for building or farmland. But forests help to balance the world's weather and climate. If we go on losing forests, global warming will get worse.

We share our world with millions of animals and plants. As the human population grows, some of the animals and plants are disappearing, and will never be seen again. People destroy **wildlife habitats** by cutting down forests and draining **wetlands**, and by using chemicals on the land. In the most crowded countries, there are only small areas of wildlife habitat left.

Wild animals depend on their natural habitats for food and shelter.

Every year, up to 27,000 species vanish forever: that is about three types of animal, insect or plant every hour. If things continue in this way, up to one fifth of all life forms on earth will disappear in the next thirty years.

This graph shows that when the population is larger, there is less wildlife habitat.

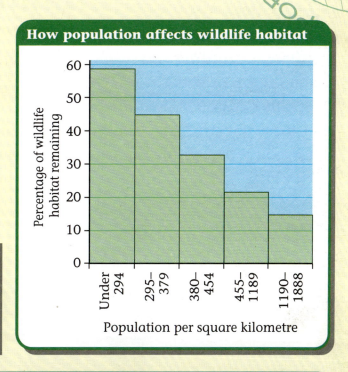

How population affects wildlife habitat

Percentage of wildlife habitat remaining vs Population per square kilometre

In danger of extinction

 34 per cent of fish

 20 per cent of reptiles

 25 per cent of mammals and amphibians

 11 per cent of birds

What can be done?

Many of the world's problems are caused by the growing number of people on the planet. We have to act now to save our planet and all the people, animals and plants that live on it.

Different countries have different ways of slowing down their population growth. In China, for example, the population growth has gone down by a half. This is because in 1979 the Chinese government said that each family was allowed to have only one child. The Chinese government helps families who have just one child, but any that have more than one child have to pay fines.

Population grows fastest in developing countries where there are lots of poor people. People have more children to help them grow crops, carry water and firewood, or work to bring money into the home.

What you can do

Rich countries, like Britain, have to help the poorest countries to become richer. In that way people won't need to have so many children. You can help by supporting charities.

The rich countries need to stop wasting resources like fuel and food. They need to be better at looking after the planet. We have to act now, if we want to stop the population clock ticking and save our planet.

Europe wastes mountains of food

Wind power does not waste resources

POP CLOCK

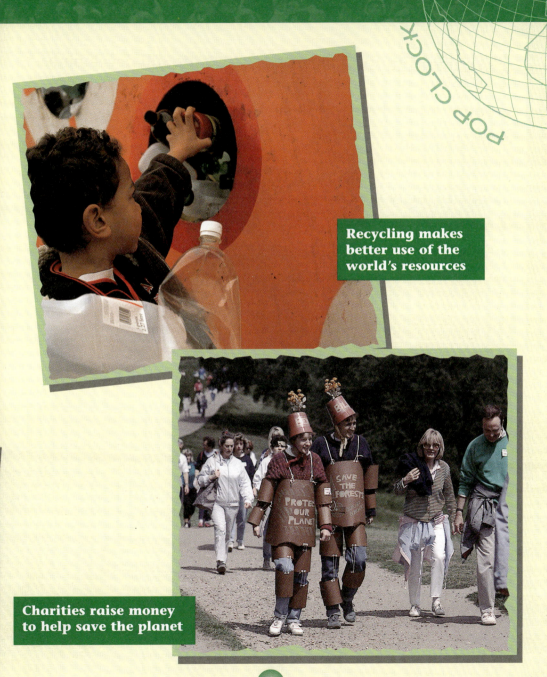

Recycling makes better use of the world's resources

Charities raise money to help save the planet

Glossary

developing countries countries which are still developing industry

drought when there is not enough rain

extinct no longer exisiting

global warming a rise in the world's temperature

megacity a city which has over 8 million people living in it

ozone layer a layer of gas in the Earth's atmosphere which protects all living things from the Sun's dangerous rays

pesticide a chemical used in farming to control unwanted insects

population clock a number count of the world's population as it grows

resources basic things that we need to live

slums poor, makeshift housing

smog polluted air

staple food the main food crop that feeds a people

wetlands watery places like marshes, river estuaries, mangrove swamps and shallow seas which are important wildlife habitats

wildlife habitat the natural home of animals, birds and insects

Further information:

Search the Internet for a 'pop clock' to get up to the minute information on world population. Some sites offer dynamics that show the world population growing in front of your eyes!

For example:

www.popinfo.org

www.popexpo.net/eMain.html

www.learner.org/exhibits/dailymath/population.html

www.ucsusa.org/resources/pop.faq.html

www.ibiblio.org/lunarbin/worldpop

Index

aid for developing countries 27

China 26
cities 14–15
consumption 20–21, 28–29
crime 16
crop damage 9

density of population 7, 25
developing countries 6–7, 27
disease 14
drought 13, 23

extinctions 4, 24

farming 9, 13
fishing 10–11
floods 23
food 8–11, 20
forests 23

global warming 22–23
grain production 8
growth of population 5, 26–27

hotspots 6–7
hunger 4, 8

jobs 14, 16–17

megacities 15
Mexico City 15

overcrowding 2–3

pollution 4, 15, 20, 22–23
population 4–5

renewable fresh water 12
resources 19, 21, 28
rich countries 28–29
Rwanda 18

shortages of fish 11
slums 15

war 18–19
water 7, 12–13
weather 4
wildlife 24–25